Who?

A DRAGON Question Book™

By Kathie Billingslea Smith
Illustrated by Robert S. Storms

A DRAGON BOOK

GRANADA

Who made the

The first rockets were invented many, many years ago in China during the 10th century. These rockets were powered by gunpowder. The gunpowder was put inside bamboo tubes to make firecrackers. Then arrows were strapped onto the firecrackers to guide them through the air to their targets.

The Chinese people used the rockets as weapons in wars. They also used them for fireworks for special celebrations. They called the rockets "arrows of fire."

irst rocket?

The rockets that we use now are very different from those simple fire arrows. Today we have huge rockets that can carry people to the moon!

Who wrote the song

Today "Happy Birthday to You" is sung more times than any other song in the world. The Apollo 9 astronauts even sang it in their space capsule in 1969, high above the earth!

This song was written by a New York teacher named Patty Smith Hill. Miss Hill loved young children and wrote the words to this song for them to sing. Her sister, Mildred J. Hill, wrote the music. At first the song was called "Good Morning to All." Later the name of the song was changed to "Happy Birthday to You." It was published in 1935 under that name.

When you next have a birthday, think of the Hill sisters as you sing their special song.

"Happy Birthday to You"?

Who are the people

Many people make the circus the greatest show on earth. Workers, called riggers, unload and set up the circus tents. Costume and set designers plan and make the fancy clothes and scenery.

Wild animal trainers work with lions and tigers and elephants — with all the performing circus animals, teaching them to jump through hoops of fire or to do other tricks.

n the circus?

High in the air above the circus, tightrope walkers balance themselves on long, thin wires. They seem to walk on thin air! Acrobats swing from trapezes, doing flips and somersaults!

The ringmaster is the circus announcer. He blows his whistle to begin and finish each circus act.

The circus clowns are favourites. They wear funny costumes and have colourful faces. Their tricks make you laugh. Underneath all their funny makeup, though, circus clowns have faces just like yours.

Who was the first

On a hot day in July of 1969, the Apollo 11 spacecraft was launched from Cape Kennedy in Florida. It was headed for the Moon! On board were three astronauts — Commander Neil Armstrong, Michael Collins, and Edwin Aldrin, Jr.

After a long trip through space lasting over four and a

person on the Moon?

half days, the Apollo 11 landing craft reached the Moon! The date was July 20, 1969. Neil Armstrong was the first one to climb out of the lander. He was dressed in a spacesuit. As he stepped onto the Moon, he said, "That's one small step for man, one giant leap for mankind."

The astronauts firmly placed an American flag on the Moon to show that they were the first people there. They studied the Moon, took many photographs, and gathered moon rocks to take back to Earth.

Who takes care of sick

When a hippo has a toothache or a monkey breaks its arm, the zoo veterinarians are the ones who come to help. Veterinarians, or "vets," as they are called, take care of animals just like doctors take care of people.

Zoo vets are busy workers. At a large zoo, they may have almost 3,000 mammals, birds, and reptiles to care for!

Zoo vets give animals check-ups. They weigh them and measure them and make sure they are eating well. They

animals in the zoo?

give sick animals medicine. Sometimes they even operate on the animals to make them feel better. This can be tricky! With a lion, doctors must first put the beast to sleep so they can get close enough to even begin the operation!

Vets keep zoo animals happy and healthy so that people can see what these special animals are like.

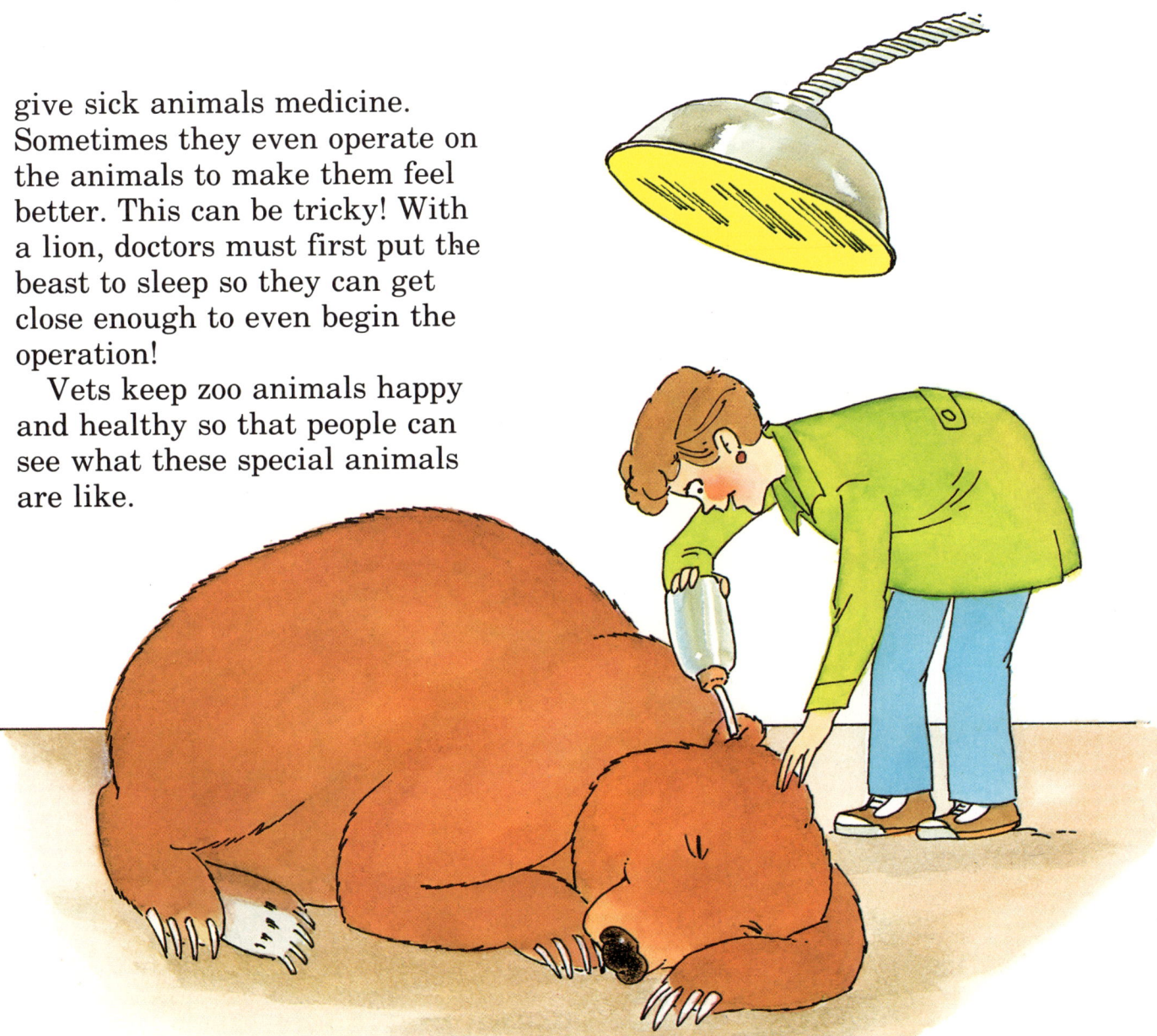

Who made the first car?

No one person can be credited with making the first car. For many years, different people tried to build a machine that could travel without horses to pull it — powered by steam or by electricity, or even by petrol, as cars are today.

The first car with a petrol-powered engine was built by Karl Benz in Germany in 1885. Mr Benz placed a petrol

engine onto a three-wheeled carriage that was shaped something like a horseshoe. He got in it, tried it, and it worked! The car travelled four times around the track by Mr Benz's factory. But the new "horseless carriage," as this early car was called, was clumsy and heavy, and it did not go very fast. Yet everyone who saw it was surprised to see a carriage that seemed to move by itself!

"Horseless carriages" were noisy and hard to steer at first. They scared people who did not understand how they worked. Sometimes people even ran away and hid when they saw a car coming!

Who sleeps during the day

Most people and animals are awake during the day. At night they go to sleep.

But some people work at night and must stay up. Police officers, firemen, doctors, and nurses often work at night to keep us safe and healthy. Some factory workers work at night to make new things we can use. During the day, these people sleep.

Many animals also "work" at night. Bats, skunks, porcupines, opossums, rats, and mice all rest during the day and become more active at night. Owls, frogs, and many insects are night animals, too. In the desert, coyotes and rattlesnakes wait until night cools the hot sands before they come out to hunt for food.

All of these animals are *nocturnal*, which means that they are up and about at night.

and stays awake at night?

Who made the firs

Charles Babbage

More than 150 years ago, an English mathematician named Charles Babbage began to build the first computer. He called it The Analytical Engine. But he was not able to finish his project. His dreams of building a computer had come too early. Some of the parts needed for his machine had not been invented.

For many years, scientists studied Mr Babbage's plans and ideas. Then, in the early 1940s, an American named Howard Aiken built the first modern electric-powered computer. It was named Mark I, but Mr Aiken nicknamed it "Babbage's Dream Come True." Mark I was huge and noisy. It was 13.7 m long, 2.4 m high, and had a million different parts. It could only do two addition problems per second.

computer?

Today's computers are much quieter and smaller than those early machines. They also work much faster. Some can do more than a million maths problems in a single second! With computers you can play your favourite computer game, draw a picture, or learn maths facts. Computers have changed our lives!

A personal computer (PC)

Mark I

Who makes the toys

Some wooden toys or stuffed animals and dolls are made by just one person. That person gets the supplies and builds or sews the toys all alone.

Most toys are made in toy factories. There many people work together to build the toys. Often each worker does just one job and then passes the toy onto the next worker. One worker might snap in the doll's head and arms, another worker might put in the legs, another might dress the doll, another might

in the toy store?

put the finished doll in the box. That way toys can be made very quickly.

If you look closely at your toys, you might be able to read where they were made. Sometimes toymakers stamp the name of their city or country onto each toy after it is finished.

Who invented the

Before telephones were invented, people could only send messages by telegraph or through the mail or by messenger.

But on March 10, 1876, all this changed. In a lab in Boston, a young inventor and teacher named Alexander Graham Bell was working on his newest invention — the telephone. He was ready to test a new *transmitter* (the part that changes your voice into electricity so it can travel over the phone wire). Accidentally, he spilled burning acid from a battery onto his clothes. "Mr Watson, come here. I want you!" Mr Bell called into his telephone.

His assistant, Thomas Watson, heard the message over his own telephone down the hall. He came running into the lab. "Mr Bell, I heard every word you said . . .!" shouted the excited Mr Watson. They had created something wonderful — the telephone!

Who made this

This book was put together by many different people.

First a writer wrote the questions and answers that would be in the book. Copies of them were sent to an editor, a typesetter, and an artist.

The *editor* read the words and then added or took away information to make the book better.

The *artist* also read the words and then drew the pictures. He left room for the words on each page.

Then the *typesetter* used a machine to put the words on

book?

special paper. These words were then placed next to the pictures. Now the pages were ready to be printed.

The *printer* made many copies of the pages. Then 24 pages and the cover were bound together to make each book . . . until

there were thousands and thousands of books.

These books were shipped to shops all across the country. People like you came to the shops to buy the books.

Have fun reading!

Who was the first person to fly?

In 1783, a French doctor named Pilâtre de Rozier flew up into the air in a balloon. He was the first person to fly. After this first flight, many other people tried ballooning, too. Balloons were rather easy to fly, but they could not be steered very well. They simply drifted with the winds. Many people worked to make a flying machine that could be steered well.

Wilbur and Orville Wright were the first to fly in an aeroplane powered by an engine. These two brothers flew their plane, *the Flyer I*, at Kitty Hawk, North Carolina, in 1903. On its first flight, the plane stayed in the air about 12 seconds and went almost 37 m. The fourth flight lasted almost a minute, and the plane travelled a distance of 260 m!

Now we have planes — great jumbo jets — that can fly for hours without stopping for fuel. They fly across oceans, and across continents as big as North America.